I0762632

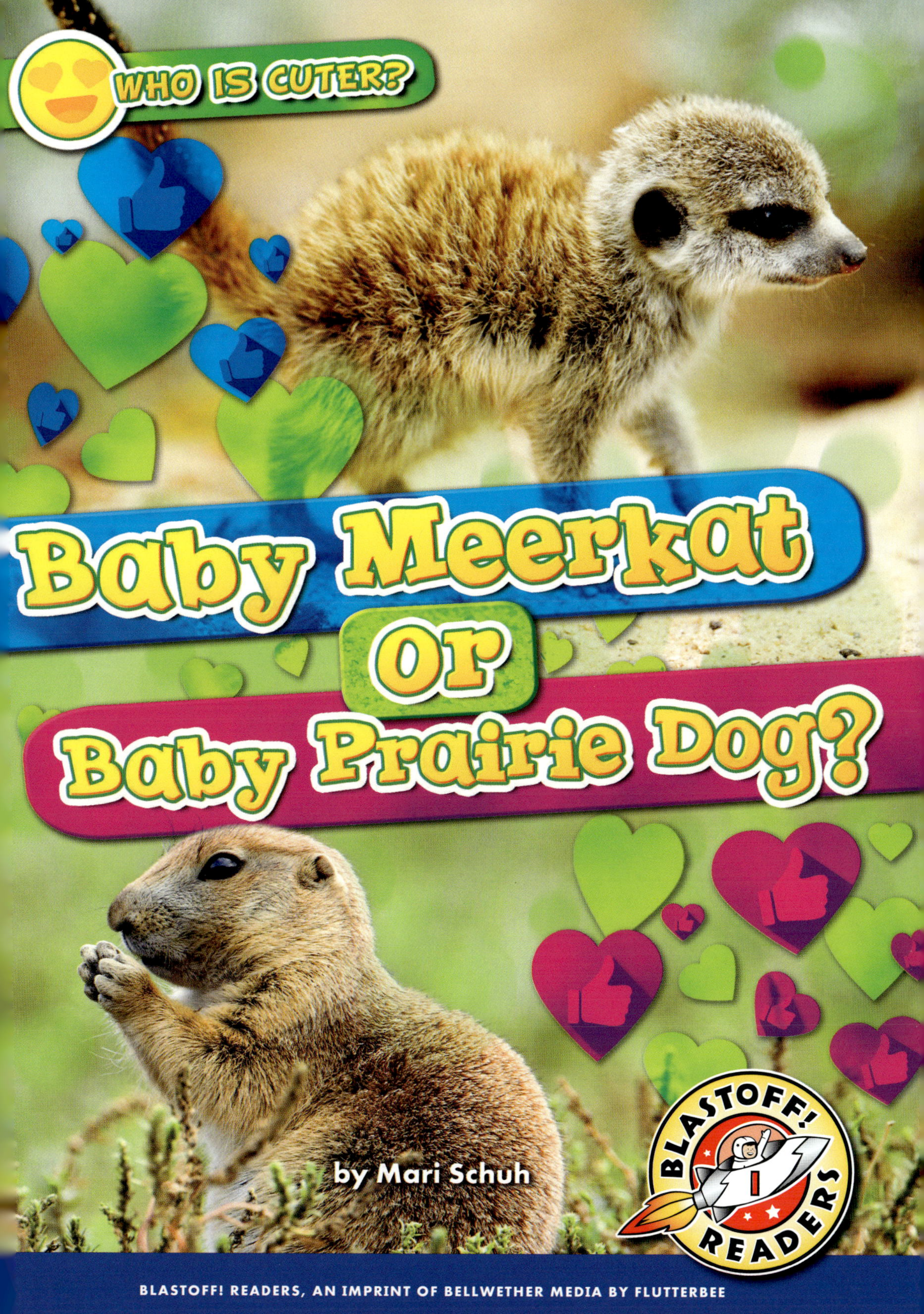
WHO IS CUTER?
Baby Meerkat
or
Baby Prairie Dog?
by Mari Schuh
BLASTOFF! READERS 1
BLASTOFF! READERS, AN IMPRINT OF BELLWETHER MEDIA BY FLUTTERBEE

Blastoff! Readers are carefully developed by literacy experts to build reading stamina and move students toward fluency by combining standards-based content with developmentally appropriate text.

Level 1 provides the most support through repetition of high-frequency words, light text, predictable sentence patterns, and strong visual support.

Level 2 offers early readers a bit more challenge through varied sentences, increased text load, and text-supportive special features.

Level 3 advances early-fluent readers toward fluency through increased text load, less reliance on photos, advancing concepts, longer sentences, and more complex special features.

★ Blastoff! Universe

Reading Level

Grade K

Grades 1–3

Grade 4

This edition first published in 2027 by Bellwether Media, Inc.

Library of Congress Cataloging-in-Publication Data

Names: Schuh, Mari, 1975- author
Title: Baby meerkat or baby prairie dog? / by Mari Schuh.
Description: Minneapolis, Minnesota : Bellwether Media, Inc, [2026] | Series: Who is cuter? | Includes bibliographical references and index. | Audience: Ages 5-8 | Audience: Grades 2-3 | Summary: "Developed by literacy experts for students in kindergarten through grade three, this book introduces baby meerkats and baby prairie dogs to young readers through leveled text and related photos"– Provided by publisher.
Identifiers: LCCN 2026001532 (print) | LCCN 2026001533 (ebook) | ISBN 9798898800246 HC | ISBN 9798898801489 eBook Subjects: LCSH: Meerkat–Infancy | Prairie dogs–Infancy
Classification: LCC QL737.C235 S34 2026 (print) | LCC QL737.C235 (ebook) | DDC 599.74/2-dc23/eng/20260220
LC record available at https://lccn.loc.gov/2026001532
LC ebook record available at https://lccn.loc.gov/2026001533

Editor: Rachael Barnes Designer: Jennifer Bowyer

Printed in the United States of America, North Mankato, MN.

Table of Contents

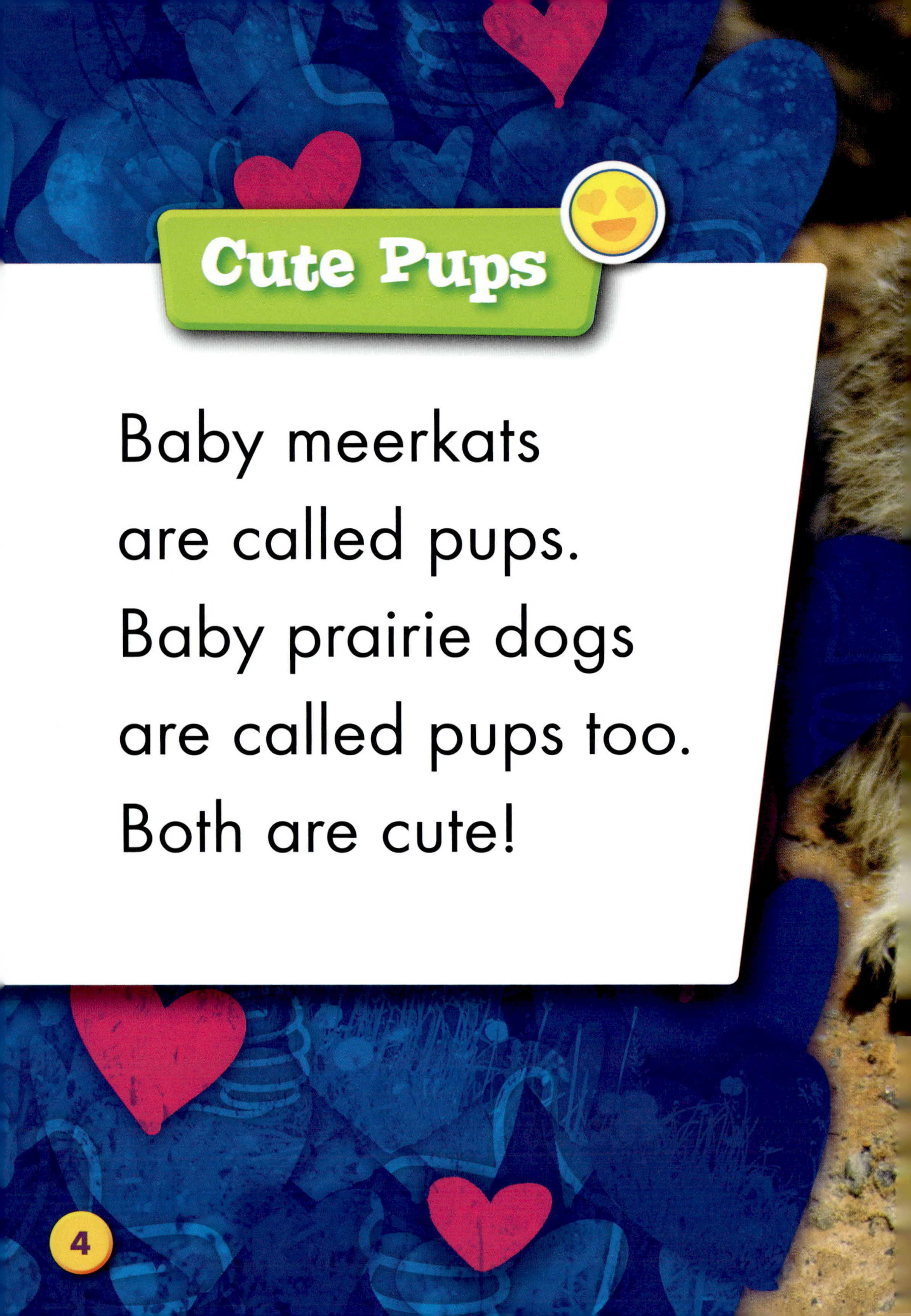

Cute Pups

Baby meerkats
are called pups.
Baby prairie dogs
are called pups too.
Both are cute!

meerkat pups
prairie dog pups

Both pups are born in **burrows**. They have **siblings**. They soon stand on their back legs.

siblings
burrow

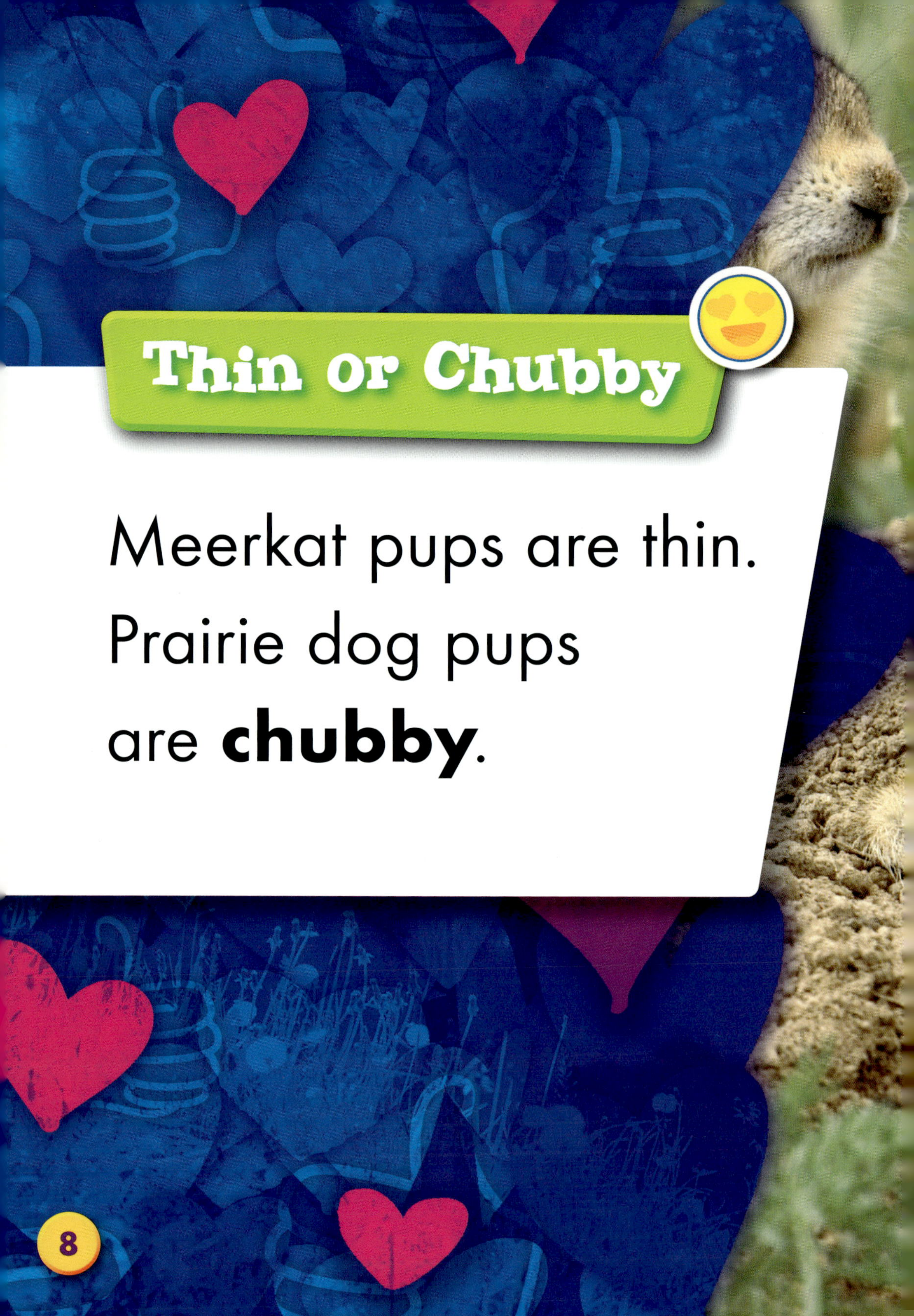

Thin or Chubby

Meerkat pups are thin.
Prairie dog pups
are **chubby**.

chubby
body

Meerkat pups have pointy **snouts**. Prairie dog pups have round snouts.

round snout
pointy snout

Prairie dog pups
have short tails.
Meerkat pups
grow long tails.

tail

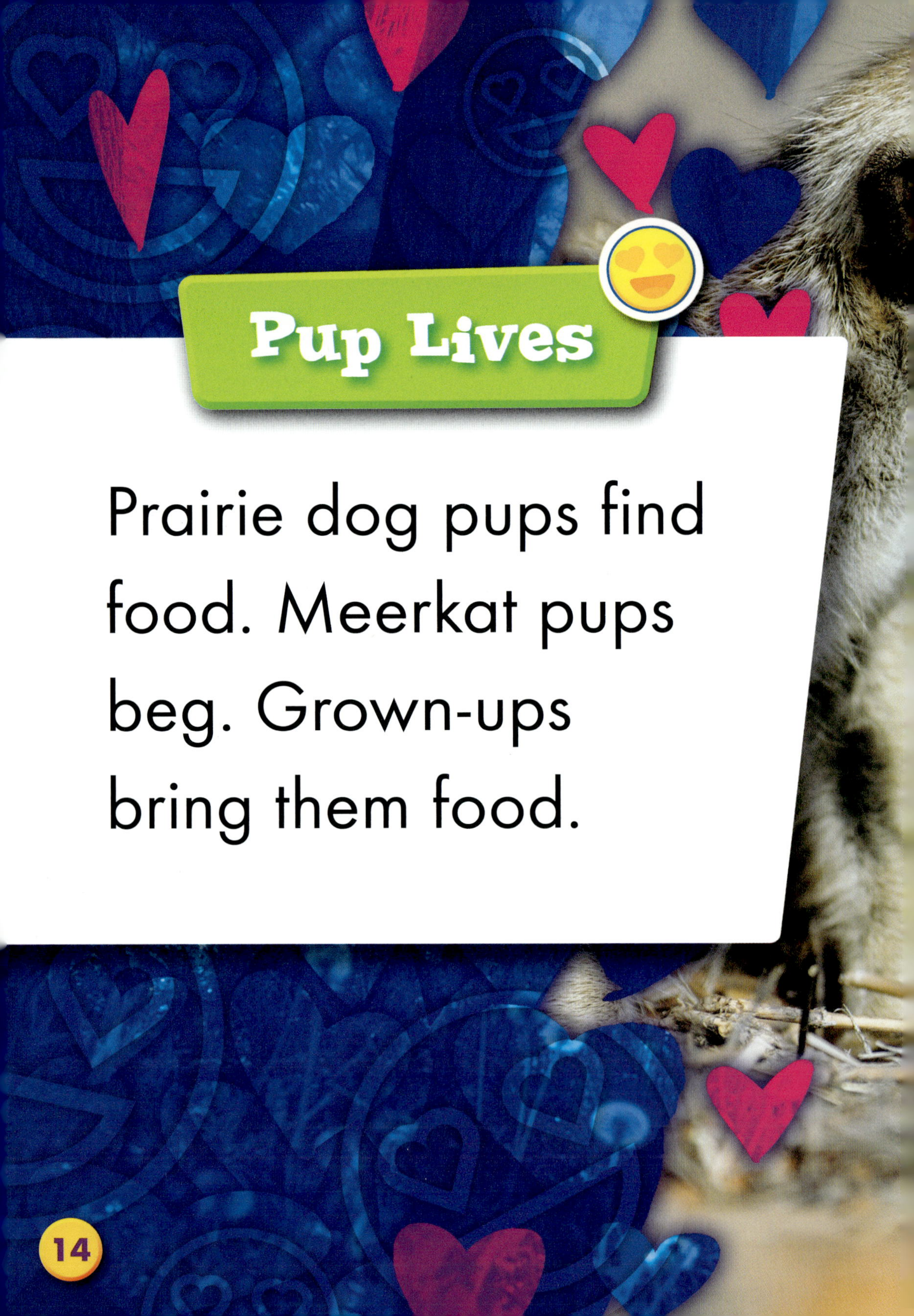

Pup Lives

Prairie dog pups find food. Meerkat pups beg. Grown-ups bring them food.

begging for food

Prairie dog pups often eat plants. Meerkat pups often eat **insects**.

insect

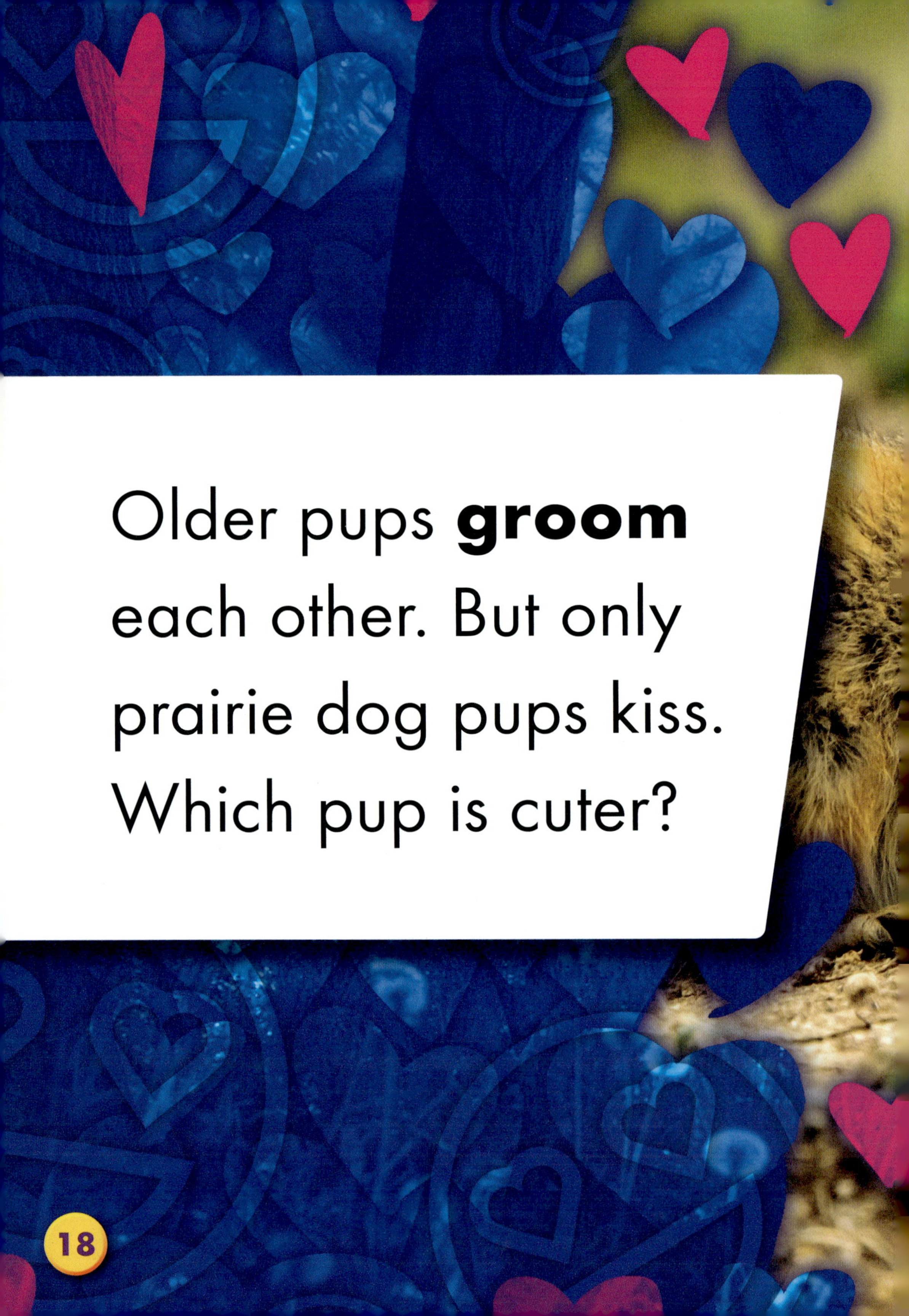

Older pups **groom** each other. But only prairie dog pups kiss. Which pup is cuter?

kissing
grooming

Who Is Cuter?

long tail

thin body

pointy snout

Baby Meerkat

begs for food

eats insects

grooms

Who is your pick?
Vote at
BellwetherMedia.com
round
snout
chubby
body
short tail
Baby Prairie Dog
finds
food
eats
plants
grooms
and
kisses

Glossary

burrows

holes or tunnels in the ground used as animals' homes

chubby

having a round, full shape

groom

to keep clean

insects

small animals with six legs and hard outer bodies

siblings

brothers and sisters

snouts

the noses and mouths of some animals

To Learn More

AT THE LIBRARY

Morlock, Rachael. *Baby Desert Animals.* Buffalo, N.Y.: PowerKids Press, 2025.

Pang, Ursula. *Prairie Dogs.* Buffalo, N.Y.: PowerKids Press, 2025.

Thompson, Kim. *Baby Prairie Dogs.* Mankato, Minn.: Creative Education and Creative Paperbacks, 2026.

ON THE WEB

FACTSURFER

Factsurfer.com gives you a safe, fun way to find more information.

1. Go to www.factsurfer.com.
2. Enter "baby meerkat or baby prairie dog" into the search box and click 🔍.
3. Select your book cover to see a list of related content.

Index

The images in this book are reproduced through the courtesy of: Image Source Limited/ Radius Images/ Alamy, front cover (meerkat); robertharding/ James Hager/ Alamy, front cover (prairie dog); Rosa Jay, pp. 3 (meerkat), 20 (main meerkat); Ger Bosma/ Alamy, p. 3 (prairie dog); Jamiesan317, pp. 4-5; liztrevathan, p. 5; imageBROKER.com/ Ingo Schulz/ Alamy, pp. 6-7; meyblume, p. 7; Max Allen/ Alamy, pp. 8-9, 22 (chubby); Lubos Kovalik, p. 9; Nature Picture Library/ Will Burrard-Lucas/ Alamy, pp. 10-11; Dennis Laughlin/ Alamy, p. 11; Nick Fox/ Alamy, pp. 12-13; IrenaSocratous, p. 13; Robin Hoskyns/ Minden Pictures, pp. 14-15; Randy Mehoves/ Alamy, pp. 15, 21 (finds food); Suzi Eszterhas/ Minden Pictures, pp. 16-17, 20 (begs for food, eats insects), 22 (insects); Jeff March/ Alamy, p. 17; Danita Delimont, pp. 18-19, 22 (snouts); Thomas Dressler/ imageBROKER, pp. 19, 20 (grooms); toos, p. 21 (main prairie dog); Paul Foulds/ Alamy, p. 21 (eats plants); imageBROKER.com/ Juergen & Christine Sohns/ Alamy, p. 21 (grooms and kisses); Jen Guyton/ Minden Pictures, p. 22 (burrows); PABimages, 22 (groom); Frank Fichtmueller, p. 22 (siblings).